YAKALOU MEDIA

GET CLARITY ABOUT YOUR CAREER

100 Questions To Ask Yourself To Find Out What You Exactly Want To Do

Contents

Disclaimer   v

I   BEFORE EVERYTHING

Introduction   3
The 5 Rules To Get The Most Out Of This Book   5
How To Use This Book   8

II   YOUR 100 QUESTIONS TO ASK YOURSELF
TO FIND OUT WHAT YOU EXACTLY WANT TO
DO

Chapter 1: Self-Assessment and Reflection   13
Exercise #1   15
Chapter 2: Career Goals and Aspirations   16
Exercise #2   18
Chapter 3: Skill Development and Education   19
Exercise #3   21
Chapter 4: Work-Life Balance   22
Exercise #4   24
Chapter 5: Networking and Relationships   26
Exercise #5   28
Chapter 6: Career Advancement   30
Exercise #6   32

Chapter 7: Job Satisfaction   34

Exercise #7   36

Chapter 8: Overcoming Challenges   38

Exercise #8   40

Chapter 9: Adaptability and Change   42

Exercise #9   44

Chapter 10: Future Planning   46

Exercise #10   48

Conclusion   50

Disclaimer

I

BEFORE EVERYTHING

Introduction

Welcome to "Get Clarity About Your Career," a guide that's more than just a book; it's a journey into the heart of your professional life. Have you ever found yourself wondering if you're on the right career path? Or perhaps you've pondered what skills you need to reach the next level in your job? This book is your companion in uncovering these answers and more.

Why is self-reflection crucial in your career? Imagine driving to a new destination without a map or GPS. You might eventually get there, but think of the unnecessary detours and frustrations along the way! Similarly, understanding your own career path requires a map, and self-reflection is the tool that helps you chart it. By asking yourself the right questions, you can reveal your true career aspirations, recognize your strengths, and identify areas for development.

Now, how should you navigate this book? It's simple. Each chapter focuses on a key aspect of career development, from understanding your personal goals to mastering the art of adaptability in a rapidly changing job market. The chapters are filled with thought-provoking questions designed to spark deep introspection and practical advice to help you take action. Don't rush through them; take your time. Reflect on each question and write down your thoughts. This isn't a race; it's a personal exploration.

Remember, this book isn't just about finding quick answers; it's about starting a conversation with yourself about your career. A conversation that is ongoing, evolving, and, most importantly, enlightening. As you turn these pages, you're taking the first step towards a more fulfilling and successful career path. Let's embark on this journey together, with clarity as our destination.

The 5 Rules To Get The Most Out Of This Book

Welcome to a chapter that's not just about reading but about making a real change. You're here because you want to transform your career, and this book is your guide. But how can you make sure you're getting the most out of it? Here are five simple rules to follow:

1. Engage Actively:

Have you ever read something and later realized you remembered nothing? That won't happen here. As you go through each chapter, engage with the material actively. Don't just read; reflect. Pause and think about how each question and piece of advice applies to you. Jot down notes, highlight what strikes you, or even talk about it with a friend. Active engagement makes the difference between reading a book and using a book.

2. Be Honest with Yourself:

This book asks questions that require honest answers. Are you ready to be truthful with yourself? Sometimes, what we need to hear isn't what we want to hear. Embrace this opportunity to be candid about your strengths, weaknesses, and true desires. It's only when we confront our real selves that we can make meaningful changes.

3. Apply What You Learn:

Have you ever learned something new and then never used that knowledge? Let's not let that happen here. This book is filled with actionable advice. Make a commitment to apply at least one thing from each chapter to your life. Whether it's a new way of thinking or a specific action, real change comes from application, not just contemplation.

4. Revisit Regularly:

Is your career static? Of course not! It's constantly evolving, and so should your understanding of it. Don't read this book just once. Keep it close and revisit chapters as you grow and your career advances. You'll find that different advice resonates at different times. This book is designed to be a lifelong career companion, not a one-time read.

5. Share and Discuss:

Ever noticed how explaining something to someone else can deepen your own understanding? Don't keep the insights you gain from this book to yourself. Share them with colleagues, friends, or mentors. Discuss your thoughts and learn from the perspectives of others. This interaction not only enriches your experience but can also open doors to new opportunities and ideas.

By following these five rules, you're not just reading a book; you're embarking on a journey of career transformation. Each page, each question, and each piece of advice is a step towards a clearer, more successful career path. Let's take these steps together, with purpose and intention. Your career clarity awaits!

How To Use This Book

Welcome to a chapter that's not just about reading but about understanding how to make the most of this journey. This book, "Get Clarity About Your Career," is not your typical read-from-front-to-back guide. It's a personal toolkit, and just like any toolkit, you don't always need every tool for every job. Sometimes, you just need a screwdriver; other times, you might require a whole set of wrenches. Similarly, this book is designed to be flexible, catering to your unique career needs at different times.

Imagine you're at a crossroads in your career. One path might lead to a promotion, another to a career change, and yet another to enhancing your current skills. You don't need the entire map when you're just deciding your next few steps. This is where the beauty of this book lies. It's segmented into focused chapters, each addressing different aspects of career development. You can jump directly to the chapter that resonates with your current situation. Feeling unsure about your career direction? Jump to the chapter on "Career Goals and Aspirations." Want to balance work with your personal life? There's a chapter on "Work-Life Balance."

Each chapter is an independent unit, filled with questions and guidance tailored to its specific theme. This structure allows you to address your immediate concerns without getting overwhelmed by the entirety of the book. It's like having a conversation with a mentor who knows exactly what to say in your particular situation. You can navigate directly to the advice you need, when you need it.

Now, you might wonder, "What if my situation changes?" That's the beauty of this book. It grows with you. As your career evolves, your needs and challenges will change. What seems irrelevant today might become crucial tomorrow. This book is here for you at every stage of your career journey. Keep it within reach, and feel free to revisit chapters as your career landscape shifts. You'll find new insights and advice each time, tailored to your evolving path.

Moreover, this isn't just a book of questions; it's a book of discovery. Each chapter encourages not just contemplation but action. You're invited to jot down thoughts, make lists, or even sketch out plans right in the margins. It's meant to be written in, dog-eared, and well-used. This interactivity ensures that the book remains relevant and personalized to your journey.

Remember, this book is not a linear narrative that you must follow from start to finish. It's a dynamic resource, adaptable to your immediate and future needs. You might find yourself drawn to a chapter on "Networking and Relationships" today and a section on "Overcoming Challenges" next month. That's perfectly fine. This book is here to serve you at the order and pace you need.

In summary, "Get Clarity About Your Career" is not just a book; it's a companion. It's here to guide, support, and grow with you throughout your career. Use it as you see fit, jump to the parts you need, and let it be your roadmap to career clarity and success. Your journey through your career is uniquely yours, and this book is here to guide you every step of the way.

II

YOUR 100 QUESTIONS TO ASK YOURSELF TO FIND OUT WHAT YOU EXACTLY WANT TO DO

Chapter 1: Self-Assessment and Reflection

Emma had always thought of herself as a dedicated nurse. Yet, during a particularly challenging shift, she found herself wondering if this was truly her calling. As she sat in the break room, exhausted, she couldn't shake off the feeling that maybe there was something else out there for her. This moment of doubt was the start of Emma's journey of self-assessment and reflection, a journey we all embark on at various points in our careers.

Self-assessment and reflection are like holding up a mirror to your professional life. It's about asking yourself the hard questions and being open to the answers, whatever they may be. For Emma, it was about understanding whether her passion for nursing was still alive or if her interests had shifted.

Now, think about where you are in your career. Are you where you want to be? Are you engaged and satisfied with your work? These aren't just rhetorical questions; they're the first step in understanding yourself better. Self-assessment is not about judging your choices harshly but about evaluating them with a kind and open heart. It's the foundation upon which you can build a career that's not just successful but also fulfilling.

To help you embark on this journey of self-discovery, here are ten straightforward questions. Take your time to ponder over them, write down your thoughts, and be honest with yourself:

1. What are three career accomplishments I'm most proud of?
2. What tasks in my current job do I enjoy the most, and why?
3. Which parts of my current job do I find challenging or unfulfilling?
4. What are my top three strengths in my professional role?
5. In what areas do I feel I need improvement or further development?
6. What have others consistently identified as my strengths and weaknesses?
7. What activities outside of work bring me the most joy and satisfaction?
8. How do my personal values align with my current career path?
9. Where do I see myself in five years, professionally?
10. What would I do if I weren't afraid of failure?

Emma's journey of reflection led her to realize that her passion for nursing was still strong, but she needed a change of environment. She eventually transitioned to a pediatric clinic, which reignited her love for nursing. Like Emma, you may find that self-assessment and reflection bring clarity, leading you to decisions that align more closely with your true professional desires and aspirations. Remember, the goal is not to find immediate answers but to start a meaningful conversation with yourself about your career.

Exercise #1

Career Timeline Exercise:

Create a timeline of your career, starting from your first job to your current position. Include key milestones, achievements, and any turning points. Once you've mapped it out, look for patterns or themes. In what moments were you the happiest? When did you feel most challenged? This visual representation can offer insights into your career progression and guide your future choices.

Chapter 2: Career Goals and Aspirations

Jason, a young graphic designer, sat in front of his computer, scrolling through his portfolio. He was proud of his work, but something felt missing. He realized he had been drifting along without any clear career direction. This was a wake-up call for Jason to start setting specific career goals and aspirations.

Setting career goals is like charting a course in a vast ocean. Without them, you're adrift, subject to the whims of the currents. With them, you have a destination and a map to guide your journey. But how do you begin to articulate these goals, especially when the future is so uncertain?

Start by thinking about what success means to you. Is it about reaching a particular position, earning a certain income, or perhaps achieving work-life balance? Understand that career goals are deeply personal and should reflect what you genuinely want, not what others expect of you.

As you ponder these aspects, here are some questions to help articulate your short-term and long-term career objectives:

1. What do I want to achieve in my career in the next year?
2. Where do I see myself professionally in five years?
3. What are my ultimate career aspirations?
4. What skills do I need to develop to reach my career goals?

5. Are there any industry-specific qualifications or experiences I should aim for?
6. How will I measure my progress towards these goals?
7. What are the potential obstacles to achieving my career goals, and how can I overcome them?
8. How do my career goals align with my personal values and lifestyle choices?
9. Who in my network can support me in achieving these goals?
10. What can I do right now to take a step towards my first goal?

After answering these questions, it's time to put your thoughts into action. Here's a practical strategy for goal-setting and achievement on the NEXT PAGE.

Jason used these strategies to set clear goals. He decided to enhance his skills through specialized courses and set a timeline to become a senior designer within three years. By defining his aspirations, Jason transformed his approach to his career, moving from aimless drifting to purposeful striving.

Your career goals and aspirations are the driving force behind your professional growth. They give you a sense of direction and motivation to overcome challenges. As you move through this chapter, keep Jason's story in mind. Remember, the journey towards achieving your career aspirations starts with a clear vision and a commitment to action. Set your goals, make them SMART, and embark on the path to turning your career aspirations into reality.

Exercise #2

SMART Goal-Setting Strategy:

Make each goal Specific, Measurable, Achievable, Relevant, and Time-bound. For example, instead of saying, "I want to be better at graphic design," a SMART goal would be, "I will complete an advanced graphic design course by the end of this quarter to enhance my design skills." This approach makes your goals clear and actionable, providing a straightforward path to follow.

Chapter 3: Skill Development and Education

Meet Sophia, a marketing manager who always felt a step behind her tech-savvy colleagues. During one team meeting, it became glaringly obvious that her lack of digital marketing knowledge was a roadblock in her career progression. This realization sparked Sophia's commitment to skill development and education, a journey that is essential for anyone looking to succeed in their career.

In today's ever-evolving job market, the only constant is change. The role of skills and education in career success cannot be overstated. They are the fuel that propels your career forward and keeps you competitive. But how do you identify which skills and knowledge you need to develop? And once identified, how do you go about acquiring them?

First, let's start by pinpointing where you currently stand. Reflect on these questions to uncover your skills and knowledge gaps:

1. What new trends or technologies are emerging in my field that I'm not familiar with?
2. Have I received feedback about areas I need to improve professionally?

3. What skills do people in my desired job position typically possess?
4. Are there any tasks at work I avoid because I lack confidence in that area?
5. What additional knowledge or education would help me excel in my current role?
6. Which of my skills are outdated or becoming less relevant in my industry?
7. What do my colleagues or competitors do better than me, and how can I learn from them?
8. Are there any certifications or courses that could significantly impact my career?
9. How do I keep up with the latest developments and trends in my industry?
10. What are my learning preferences (e.g., online courses, workshops, books)?

Sophia embraced these strategies and enrolled in digital marketing courses. She dedicated time each week to learning and applying her new knowledge in her role. Gradually, she transformed from a marketing manager who struggled with digital trends to a leader in her team's digital strategies.

Skill development and education are not just about filling gaps; they're about empowering yourself to reach new heights in your career. As you work through this chapter, think of Sophia's journey. Remember, the pursuit of knowledge is a lifelong journey, and every step you take in learning and development is a step towards a more successful and fulfilling career.

Exercise #3

Develop These Skills:

Identifying your gaps is just the beginning. The next step is actively seeking ways to develop these skills. Here are some tips for skill development and continuous learning:

1. Leverage Online Resources: The internet is a treasure trove of knowledge. Explore online courses, webinars, and tutorials that align with your career needs.
2. Attend Workshops and Seminars: These can provide in-depth knowledge and hands-on experience, as well as opportunities to network with industry peers.
3. Read Widely: Stay informed about your industry by reading books, journals, and articles. This habit will keep you updated and inspire new ideas.
4. Seek Mentorship: A mentor who is experienced in your field can provide guidance, insights, and advice that's invaluable for your growth.
5. Set Learning Goals: Just like career goals, set specific, measurable, and time-bound goals for your learning and development.

Chapter 4: Work-Life Balance

Consider the story of Alex, a software engineer who was a star at his job but struggled to find time for his family and hobbies. Working late nights and weekends, Alex's health and personal relationships began to suffer. His story underscores a vital lesson: achieving a healthy work-life balance is crucial, not just for personal happiness but also for professional success.

The importance of balancing a career and personal life can't be overstated. It's like walking a tightrope; lean too much on one side, and you risk falling off. But how do you assess your current work-life balance? And more importantly, how can you improve it?

To get started, reflect on these questions:

1. How often do I work beyond my official working hours?
2. Do I frequently think about work during my personal time?
3. How much quality time do I spend with my family and friends?
4. Am I able to pursue hobbies or interests outside of work?
5. Do I feel constantly drained or stressed because of work?
6. How often do I take breaks or vacations?
7. Do I find it difficult to disconnect from work-related communications after hours?

8. How satisfied am I with my current work-life balance?
9. Does my job leave me enough time for self-care and relaxation?
10. What changes can I make to improve my work-life balance?

Alex took these steps to heart. He started by setting firm boundaries at work and communicating openly with his manager about his need for balance. He began scheduling regular time for his hobbies and family, which not only improved his personal life but also made him more productive and satisfied at work.

Work-life balance is not just about dividing your time evenly; it's about finding a rhythm that allows you to thrive both at work and at home. As you delve into this chapter, remember Alex's story. It's a reminder that work is just one part of life, and nurturing all aspects of your life is key to overall success and happiness.

Exercise #4

Healthy Balance:

After you've pondered these questions, consider these practical tips for achieving a healthy balance:

1. Set Boundaries: Establish clear limits on your work time and personal time. Learn to say no when work demands infringe on your personal life.
2. Prioritize Your Health: Make time for exercise, adequate sleep, and healthy eating. Your physical and mental health are foundational to both career success and personal well-being.
3. Time Management: Use tools and techniques to manage your time effectively. Prioritize tasks and avoid procrastination.
4. Unplug Regularly: Take regular breaks from technology, especially work emails and calls during your off-hours.
5. Pursue Hobbies: Engage in activities outside of work that make you happy. This can be an excellent way to decompress and find fulfillment.
6. Seek Support: Don't hesitate to ask for help when needed,

either at work or home. Delegating tasks can free up your time and reduce stress.

7. Regular check-ins: Continuously assess your work-life balance and make adjustments as necessary. It's an ongoing process, not a one-time fix.

Chapter 5: Networking and Relationships

Imagine Lisa, a talented but introverted accountant who always shied away from networking events. Despite her expertise, she found herself overlooked for opportunities that often went to more well-connected colleagues. Lisa's realization that professional networking and relationships are indispensable for career advancement marked a turning point in her journey.

The value of professional networking cannot be understated. It's not just about collecting business cards or adding connections on LinkedIn; it's about building meaningful relationships that can open doors to new opportunities, provide support, and foster career growth. But how can you evaluate and improve your networking skills, especially if, like Lisa, you find networking daunting?

To start enhancing your networking skills, reflect on these questions:

1. How often do I attend networking events or professional gatherings?
2. Do I have a clear purpose when I network, or do I just 'go with the flow'?
3. How comfortable do I feel initiating conversations with

new people?

4. Do I follow up with new contacts after meeting them?
5. What strategies do I use to maintain my existing professional relationships?
6. How diverse is my professional network in terms of industries, roles, and experiences?
7. Do I actively seek opportunities to help others in my network?
8. How effectively do I use social media and professional platforms for networking?
9. Have I ever experienced the benefits of a strong professional network?
10. What are my biggest challenges or fears regarding networking?

Lisa took these strategies to heart. She started by attending local networking events, initially just as an observer. Gradually, she began to engage more, initiating conversations and following up with new contacts. Over time, she built a robust network, leading to new career opportunities and collaborations.

Networking and building professional relationships are about making genuine connections that can mutually benefit everyone involved. As you explore this chapter, think of Lisa's transformation. It's a reminder that even the most reserved individuals can become effective networkers, opening new doors and paving the way for career success.

Exercise #5

Build Professional Connections:

After pondering these questions, consider adopting these strategies to build and maintain professional connections:

1. Be Purposeful: Approach networking with clear objectives. Know what you want to achieve, whether it's finding a mentor, learning about new industry trends, or seeking job opportunities.
2. Practice Active Listening: Networking is as much about listening as it is about talking. Show genuine interest in others' experiences and viewpoints.
3. Follow Up: After meeting someone, send a follow-up message to express your appreciation for the conversation and to keep the connection alive.
4. Offer Value: Networking is a two-way street. Think about how you can help others in your network, not just what you can gain.
5. Diversify Your Network: Expand your network beyond your immediate industry or role. Diverse connections can offer fresh perspectives and unexpected opportunities.

6. Use Social Media Wisely: Platforms like LinkedIn can be powerful networking tools. Engage with content, join relevant groups, and share your insights.
7. Regular Engagement: Keep in touch with your network through occasional messages, sharing useful information, or congratulating them on their achievements.

Chapter 6: Career Advancement

Meet Carlos, a dedicated junior analyst with big dreams. Despite his hard work, he felt stuck in the same role for years. His story reflects a common dilemma: understanding the pathway to career growth and learning how to navigate it effectively. It's not just about working hard; it's about working smart and recognizing the right opportunities.

Career advancement is a strategic journey. It involves under-standing where you want to go and mapping out the steps to get there. But how do you begin to chart this path? And once you have a plan, how do you put it into action?

Begin by contemplating these questions to guide your career progression:

1. What does career advancement mean to me?
2. What are the key milestones I want to achieve in my career?
3. What skills and experiences are required for the next step in my career?
4. Who are the people in my network that can help me advance in my career?
5. Have I sought feedback on my performance and areas for improvement?
6. What additional responsibilities can I take on to demon-

strate my readiness for advancement?

7. How do I stay updated with industry trends and advancements?

8. What barriers or challenges am I facing in advancing my career, and how can I overcome them?

9. How do I market myself for the roles or opportunities I aspire to?

10. What are the specific actions I can take in the next six months to move closer to my career goals?

Carlos realized that he needed to be more proactive in seeking growth opportunities. He started by requesting more challenging projects and showcasing his successes to his supervisors. He also expanded his network by connecting with industry professionals and joining professional associations. These steps not only increased his visibility but also provided him with valuable insights into his career path.

Career advancement is a proactive and ongoing process. As you delve into this chapter, keep Carlos's story in mind. It's a testament to the fact that advancement isn't just about time served or hard work; it's about strategic actions, continuous learning, and building the right relationships. Your pathway to career growth is yours to forge.

Exercise #6

Making Impactful Moves:

With these questions in mind, consider these tips for seeking opportunities and making impactful moves:

1. Seek Feedback and Act on It: Regularly ask for feedback from peers, supervisors, and mentors. Use this feedback constructively to improve and prepare for advancement.
2. Expand Your Skill Set: Continuously learn and acquire new skills that are valuable for your desired career path. Consider certifications, training, or further education.
3. Build a Strong Network: Cultivate relationships with individuals both inside and outside your organization. A strong network can provide support, advice, and access to opportunities.
4. Be Proactive: Don't wait for opportunities to come to you. Seek them out, whether it's volunteering for new projects, proposing innovative ideas, or applying for higher positions.
5. Showcase Your Achievements: Ensure that your contributions are visible to decision-makers. Don't be shy

about sharing your successes and how they impact the organization.

6. Stay Informed: Keep abreast of industry trends, changes, and job requirements. Being informed positions you as a knowledgeable and proactive professional.

Chapter 7: Job Satisfaction

Imagine Sarah is a project manager at a bustling tech company. Despite a successful career and a commendable paycheck, she often felt a lack of fulfillment at work. Sarah's situation is not uncommon. Many professionals find themselves questioning their job satisfaction and seeking ways to derive more joy and contentment from their work.

Job satisfaction is a complex blend of various factors; it's about feeling valued, finding purpose in your work, and having a sense of accomplishment. But how do you assess your level of job satisfaction? And what can you do to enhance it?

To start evaluating your job satisfaction, consider these reflective questions:

1. Do I feel enthusiastic about going to work most days?
2. What aspects of my job do I enjoy the most, and why?
3. Do I feel that my work contributes to something meaning-ful?
4. How appreciated and recognized do I feel in my workplace?
5. Am I able to use my strengths and skills effectively in my role?
6. How well do my values align with my company's culture and mission?

7. Do I have a good balance between challenging and reward-ing tasks?

8. How do I feel about the relationships I have with my colleagues and superiors?

9. Are there growth and learning opportunities available to me in my current role?

10. What changes could make my job more satisfying and fulfilling?

Sarah took proactive steps to improve her job satisfaction. She started by identifying aspects of her job that she loved and seeking out more projects in those areas. She also made an effort to build stronger relationships with her team. These changes, combined with a renewed focus on work-life balance, significantly improved her sense of fulfillment at work.

Job satisfaction is crucial for a rewarding career. As you explore this chapter, think of Sarah's journey as an example of how assessing and actively working on various aspects of your job can lead to a more satisfying and fulfilling career. Remember, job satisfaction is not just about the role you play; it's also about how you perceive and engage with your work.

Exercise #7

Job Satisfaction:

After pondering these questions, here are some tips for increasing job satisfaction:

1. Seek Meaningful Work: Look for tasks and projects that align with your interests and values. Feeling that your work is meaningful can significantly boost job satisfaction.
2. Cultivate Positive Relationships: Strong connections with colleagues can improve your work environment. Engage in team activities and build supportive relationships.
3. Ask for Feedback: Regular feedback can help you understand your impact and areas for growth, contributing to a sense of accomplishment and direction.
4. Pursue Professional Development: Continuously seek opportunities for learning and growth. It can be through formal education, workshops, or taking on new challenges at work.
5. Voice Your Needs: If there are aspects of your job that are causing dissatisfaction, communicate with your superiors. Sometimes small changes can make a big difference.

6. Focus on Work–Life Balance: Ensuring a healthy balance between your professional and personal lives is key to overall job satisfaction.
7. Practice Gratitude: Acknowledge and appreciate the positive aspects of your job. A shift in perspective can sometimes make a significant difference in how you feel about your work.

Chapter 8: Overcoming Challenges

Meet David, an ambitious young professional in the field of marketing. His career was on a steady rise until he encountered a major setback: a project he led did not meet expectations and resulted in significant client dissatisfaction. This challenge tested David's resilience and problem-solving abilities, highlighting an essential aspect of professional growth: overcoming challenges.

Every career is strewn with obstacles, from unexpected project hurdles to workplace conflicts. How you navigate these challenges can define your career trajectory. But what are the common career obstacles, and how can you develop strategies to overcome them?

To begin addressing career challenges, reflect on these questions:

1. What are the most significant challenges I have faced in my career so far?
2. How did I handle these challenges, and what was the outcome?
3. Are there patterns in the types of obstacles I encounter at work?
4. How do I typically react to stressful or challenging situa-

tions on the job?

5. What resources (people, tools, and knowledge) do I turn to when faced with a professional hurdle?
6. Have I avoided certain opportunities or tasks due to fear of failure or difficulty?
7. How do I seek help or feedback when faced with a challenge?
8. What can past failures teach me about overcoming future obstacles?
9. How resilient do I feel in the face of setbacks?
10. What strategies can I implement to improve my problem-solving skills?

David took these insights to heart. He analyzed where the project had gone wrong, sought feedback, and took responsibility for the missteps. He used this experience as a learning opportunity, which not only helped him in future projects but also earned him respect from his peers and superiors.

Overcoming challenges is an integral part of a successful career. As you work through this chapter, keep David's story in mind. It's a testament to the fact that while obstacles are inevitable, they can also be the stepping stones to greater professional success and personal growth. Remember, it's not the challenges that define you, but how you overcome them.

Exercise #8

Problem-Solving Exercise:

As you ponder these questions, consider adopting these strategies for resilience and problem-solving:

1. Develop a Growth Mindset: View challenges as opportunities to learn and grow rather than as insurmountable obstacles.
2. Build a Support Network: Cultivate relationships with mentors, peers, and colleagues who can offer guidance and support.
3. Stay Calm and Analytical: In the face of a challenge, take a step back to assess the situation calmly and objectively.
4. Be Proactive: Don't wait for a problem to escalate. Address issues early on and seek solutions actively.
5. Learn from Failures: Every setback has a lesson. Reflect on what went wrong and how it can inform your future decisions.
6. Enhance Your Skill Set: Continuously upgrade your skills to better equip yourself for unexpected challenges.
7. Practice Resilience: Resilience is like a muscle; it gets

stronger with practice. Embrace small challenges to build your resilience over time.

Chapter 9: Adaptability and Change

Consider the story of Angela, a seasoned marketing director at a traditional retail firm. When the industry started shifting towards digital and e-commerce, Angela faced a critical choice: adapt or remain in the comfort of the familiar. Her decision to embrace change and adapt her skills is a powerful testament to the importance of adaptability in a rapidly evolving work environment.

Adaptability is not just about surviving change; it's about thriving in it. It's the ability to be flexible, learn new skills, and adjust your mindset in the face of changing circumstances. But how do you assess your own adaptability? And what steps can you take to become more adaptable and open to new opportunities?

Begin by exploring these questions to gauge your adaptability:

1. How do I usually respond to significant changes at work?
2. Can I recall a time when I successfully adapted to a new situation or role?
3. What are my initial feelings towards change—excitement, fear, or resistance?
4. How quickly do I adjust to new procedures, technologies, or environments?

5. Am I proactive in learning new skills or do I wait until it becomes a necessity?
6. How do I handle uncertainty or ambiguity in my job?
7. Do I actively seek feedback to improve and adapt my work?
8. In what ways have I been innovative or creative in solving problems at work?
9. How often do I step out of my comfort zone to try new things?
10. What strategies can I use to become more adaptable in my career?

Angela's willingness to adapt led her to enroll in digital marketing courses and actively participate in industry forums. This not only expanded her skill set but also reinvigorated her career, allowing her to lead her company's transition into the digital age successfully.

In today's fast-paced world, adaptability is a crucial skill for career success. As you delve into this chapter, think of Angela's journey. It's a reminder that embracing change and staying flexible can open new doors and create exciting opportunities. Your ability to adapt is not just about keeping up; it's about leading the way in your career.

Exercise #9

Adaptability Exercise:

Now, let's look at some tips for enhancing your adaptability:

1. Embrace a Learning Mindset: View every change as an opportunity to learn something new. Stay curious and open-minded.
2. Stay Informed: Keep up with industry trends, emerging technologies, and market shifts. This knowledge can help you anticipate and adapt to changes more effectively.
3. Cultivate Flexibility: Be open to new ways of doing things. Flexibility is key in adapting to new situations and challenges.
4. Build a Diverse Network: A network with varied perspectives can provide insights and support as you navigate change.
5. Develop Resilience: Resilience will help you recover quickly from setbacks and stay focused on your goals.
6. Practice Mindfulness: Mindfulness techniques can improve your ability to remain calm and clear-headed in the face of change.

7. Take Initiative: Don't wait for change to happen to you. Be proactive in seeking out new opportunities and experiences.

Chapter 10: Future Planning

Meet Raj, an IT specialist with a passion for innovation. As he observed rapid advancements in technology, Raj realized the importance of future planning in his career. He knew that staying relevant in his fast-evolving field required anticipation, preparation, and adaptability to upcoming trends and technologies.

Future planning is about looking ahead and preparing for what's next. It's about understanding where your industry is headed and aligning your career trajectory accordingly. But how do you anticipate future trends, and what steps can you take to ensure long-term career success?

To begin your journey of future planning, consider these reflective questions:

1. What emerging trends are likely to impact my industry in the next five to ten years?
2. How can I align my current skill set with these future trends?
3. What additional skills or knowledge will I need to stay relevant and competitive?
4. Who are the thought leaders or innovators in my field, and how can I learn from them?

5. Are there upcoming technologies or methodologies I should be familiar with?
6. How does my current career plan align with projected industry developments?
7. What networking opportunities can I pursue to connect with forward-thinking professionals?
8. How often do I review and update my career goals based on industry changes?
9. What are the potential risks in my field, and how can I prepare for them?
10. How can I contribute to the future development of my industry or profession?

Raj took proactive steps by enrolling in courses on emerging technologies and actively participating in industry think tanks. This not only kept him informed but also positioned him as a valuable resource in his organization, ready to lead new initiatives.

Future planning is a dynamic process that requires ongoing attention and action. As you work through this chapter, consider Raj's proactive approach. It's a reminder that by anticipating and preparing for future trends, you not only secure your own career progression but also contribute to shaping the future of your field. Your journey into the future of your career starts with the steps you take today.

Exercise #10

Career Trends Exercise:

With these questions in mind, let's explore some strategies for staying relevant and preparing for future career trends:

1. Continuous Learning: Commit to lifelong learning to keep your skills and knowledge up-to-date. This might include formal education, online courses, workshops, or self-study.
2. Stay Informed: Regularly read industry publications, follow relevant blogs or podcasts, and attend conferences or webinars to stay abreast of new developments.
3. Network Proactively: Build relationships with peers, mentors, and industry leaders who can provide insights into future trends and opportunities.
4. Be Open to Change: Cultivate an attitude of flexibility and openness to new ideas and approaches. Be willing to adapt to changing circumstances and technologies.
5. Develop Soft Skills: In addition to technical skills, focus on enhancing soft skills like creativity, critical thinking, and emotional intelligence, which are crucial in adapting

to future changes.

6. Experiment and Innovate: Don't be afraid to experiment with new ideas or technologies in your current role. Innovation is key to staying ahead in any field.

7. Plan and Review: Regularly review your career plan to ensure it aligns with both your personal goals and the evolving landscape of your industry.

Conclusion

As we reach the end of "Get Clarity About Your Career," I want to extend my heartfelt gratitude to you, the reader. Your dedication to exploring this book is not just a testament to your commitment to personal growth but also a step towards realizing your full potential in your career journey.

Throughout these chapters, we've navigated various aspects of professional development, from self-assessment and goal-setting to overcoming challenges and planning for the future. The key takeaways are clear: understand yourself, set meaningful goals, embrace continuous learning, build strong networks, and stay adaptable in an ever-changing work environment. These principles are the pillars upon which a successful and fulfilling career is built.

But remember, this is not the end of your journey; it's just the beginning. The world of work is constantly evolving, and so should you. Keep this book as a guide, revisit chapters as you grow, and continue to apply its lessons to your life. Your career is a unique path that you carve for yourself, filled with opportunities and possibilities.

As you move forward, I encourage you to share your thoughts about this book. Your review is not just feedback for me; it's a beacon for others who are seeking guidance in their career paths.

Your insights and experiences can help illuminate the way for them, just as this book has hopefully illuminated a path for you.

By leaving a review, you're contributing to a larger community of career seekers and change-makers. You're helping others find this resource, which might be the key they need to unlock their career potential. Your words have the power to inspire, motivate, and encourage someone out there who might be standing at a career crossroads, unsure of which way to turn.

I thank you again for joining me on this journey. Remember, your career is a canvas of endless possibilities, and you are the artist. Here's to your continued success and fulfillment as you paint your professional future with the vibrant colors of your skills, passions, and dreams. Let your review be the stroke that helps others begin their masterpiece.